A writer's labours

I was working on the proof of my poems all this morning and took out
a comma.
In the afternoon I put it back again.

Oscar Wilde

Home Visits

In November 2019 The Times published a series of letters relating to GP home visits. My good friend David Haslam had the following letter published.

Sir,
I have always believed that some GP home visits are justified on medical grounds. However, during one harsh winter I recall a patient asking for a home visit to her isolated country cottage. I politely asked if she was not well enough to get to the surgery. "Oh no," she said. "That would be quite impossible. It's the snow, the road is completely blocked".

Sir David Haslam, FSBC

This reminded me of a nocturnal home visit request in my own practice in Suffolk.

When asked for the reason for the request the patient replied "Oh, our condom has split and we would be grateful if you would supply a replacement".

Some years ago, my brother-in-law Neil Doherty received the following letter from his local Hertfordshire council regarding Rights of Way.

Dear Sir,

Thank you for your application. Unfortunately, a couple of minor amendments are required.

The first amendment is required in box 4 of Part A.

The second amendment is on Part C.

Paragraph 4 is not necessary as it refers to a previous statutory declaration. In the old system of Section 31 deposits, you would first make a statement, which would be followed up within 10 years by a statutory declaration.

This is now replaced by a statement made on Part A which is followed up within 20 years by a declaration on Part C, which is no longer sworn. Therefore you are correct in paragraph 3 of Part C by referring to your statement, but you then need to remove Paragraph 4, as your current application is your equivalent of the statutory declaration.

I hope this is clear.

Yours sincerely

A batsman caught short

Colin Cowdrey, the great Kent and England batsman, has a plaque in the precincts of Canterbury Cathedral commemorating his last visit to the city in 2000. He was being taken to King's School but had been delayed in traffic. In desperation he asked his driver to stop so that he could pop out for a brief moment behind a tree.

This visit to the precinct is recorded on the plaque with an inscription in Latin:

Claviger hic dominus metam non contigit aptam cowdreius sed mox exonoratus abit.

Translated:
"Here Cowdrey, master of the bat, failed to reach the crease but soon left relieved."

Ecumenism

A new regular cricket fixture is that between the Archbishop of Canterbury's X1 and a Vatican X1. After the 2019 fixture the Church of England held a 3-2 lead in the series. Last year the Anglicans included two women team members, an option not available to the Catholics.

Excitement at Lord's

2020 is the 150th anniversary of probably the most exciting Varsity match.
10,000 spectators watched the close of the match with Oxford requiring three runs to win off the final three balls.
Cambridge's Frank Cobden then proceeded to take a hat-trick to win the match for the light-blues.

No Postcodes

Sir,
The best return address delivered to our company was from a
gentleman at "Third cottage (red door), near the windsock, Stornoway.

Letter to the Times, March 2020

Sir,
Further to the letters about partial addresses, a number of years ago I
sent a postcard from France to "The front four seats on the second
carriage of the 07.47 from Wolverton to London Euston". I am pleased
to report that it arrived safely via the train guard.

Letter to the Times, March 2020

Class distinction

"I divide my officers into four classes; the clever, the lazy, the industrious and the stupid. Each officer possesses at least two of these qualities. Those who are clever and industrious are fitted for the highest staff appointments. Use can be made of those who are stupid and lazy. The man who is clever and lazy, however, is for the very highest command; he has the temperament and nerves to deal with all situations. But whoever is stupid and industrious is a menace and must be removed immediately".

General Kurt von Hammerstein-Equord, Head of the German Army in 1930 and an opponent of Hitler and the Nazi party

Notes from the front line

An actual consultation on Covid-19 in Galway:

Doctor: "You'll need to self-isolate until you are tested and get the result."
Patient: "OK. I understand. Will they call me before they come over to make sure I'm in?"

Thanks to Jim Cox

The necessities

During the panic-buying / hoarding phase of the Covid-19 pandemic in March, the following observation was made:
Standing at the checkout, there was a gentleman with a large trolley full of just one item. 48 jars of marmalade.

Face-mask protocol

In its edition for July 31st 2020, 'Private Eye' included the following passage in its MD column.
Masks do not reduce your oxygen saturation but they only work if used correctly, and yet many spectacle-wearers steam up and lower the mask below the nose, which is akin to wearing underpants with your penis on the outside. Repeatedly touching your mask (or your penis) is poor infection control, as is leaving it around on the sideboard after use.

Thanks to Jim Cox

75 years on

Libby Calder a friend of my sister, Barbara, advised me she had read the following account of a woman who was remembering celebrating VE Day, 8th May 1945.

"When the war ended we all went to the pub to celebrate, we got so drunk that when we came out we had to drive home."

Life or death

My cousin Tony Crouch, a retired publisher, who for many years lived and worked in California and then moved to Colorado, sent me the following true account of a potentially ticklish legal issue related to a prison inmate's demise.

An Iowa court ruled against an inmate who claimed he completed his life sentence by briefly dying. He was serving a life sentence for murder, and was resuscitated after his heart stopped.
He argued that his 'death' qualified him for release.
The court was unpersuaded. 'He is either still alive' wrote the judge, 'in which case he must remain in prison, or he is actually dead, in which case this appeal is moot.'

This reminded me of a Suffolk General Practitioner some years ago.

Since the advent of the NHS, GPs have been independent contractors of services to the Government, not salaried employees. The GP contract, as might be imagined, has been somewhat complex, subject to periodic bilateral revision, but on the whole not open to interpretation. If a GP was called out to undertake a night visit to a patient's home between the hours of 10pm and 7am he was entitled to claim a night visit fee. The doctor in question was called out having been advised that a patient had died. It was necessary for him to confirm death before any further action could be taken. He duly visited, confirmed death, and the next morning submitted a claim for the fee.

His fee claim was rejected by the Suffolk Family Practitioner Committee, (the government NHS agency) on the grounds that as the patient was dead, a visit was not required. The GP responded to the rejection, arguing that as the patient was not legally dead until death had been confirmed by a medical practitioner following appropriate examination, the patient was still officially alive until the night visit had been completed.

The fee was paid.

Heredity

I am the family face;
Flesh perishes, I live on,
Projecting trait and trace
Through time to times anon,
And leaping from place to place
Over oblivion.
The years-heired feature that can
In curve and voice and eye
Despise the human span
Of durance – that is I
The eternal thing in man,
That heeds no call to die.

Thomas Hardy, 1917

All eventualities catered for!

A late 19th century advertisement from FREDERICK & Co - Complete Mountaineering Outfitters - included amongst other items the following:

Glacier lantern, folding, for the pocket.
Spiral puttees, all shades.
Light slippers, folding, for the pocket.
Sandals for wading.
Ice axes.
Red Strand Alpine Club ropes.
English picks.
Bernese rucksacks.
Snow spectacles.
Crutches and sticks to measure.
Artificial legs and arms made to order.

Thanks to Jim Cox

Foreign relations

Friday 18th October 2019
The then President of the European Commission, Jean Claude Juncker, gave a press conference, following the latest Brexit agreement with the British Government. He opened with the following words:

"This press conference will be in English, as everyone understands English............. but no one understands England."

Why English is hard to learn

We'll begin with the box; plural is boxes,
But the plural of ox is oxen, not oxes.
One fowl is a goose, and two are called geese,
Yet the plural of moose is never called meese.

You may find a lone mouse or a house full of mice,
But the plural of house is houses, not hice,
The plural of man is always men,
But the plural of pan is never pen.

If I speak of a foot, and you show me two feet,
And I give you a book, would a pair be a beek?
If one is a tooth and a whole set are teeth,
Why shouldn't two booths be called beeth.

If the singular is this and the plural are these,
Should the plural of kiss be ever called keese.

We speak of a brother and also of brethren,
But though we say mother, we never say methren,
Then the masculine pronouns are he, his and him;
But imagine the feminine…. She, shis and shim.

Anonymous. Thanks to Josh Winter

From the BBC

The BBC Radio 4 News Quiz celebrated its 100th series with 100 seconds of listeners' news quotes – a selection:

A scaffolder was unaware that he had shot himself in the head with a rivet gun until he went to the canteen and couldn't take his hard hat off.

Animal lovers broke into a car in Whangarei, New Zealand, to rescue a dog locked in the back. It was a stuffed dog to deter people from breaking into the car.

A man in his forties remains in hospital after suffering injuries when he was shot twice in the Jolly Roger in the early hours of Saturday morning.

Would the congregation please note that the bowl at the back of the church labelled 'For the sick' is for monetary donations only.

A new study suggests that being given a flu jab in the morning is more effective than being given one in the afternoon.

The Pope's representative in Britain, the Apostolic Nuncio, has visited Cardiff to reassure the clergy and the laity of the Arch-Diocese in the wake of the conviction for sex offences of two priests. This afternoon he will meet with a group of nuns and lay people.

This evening the thunderstorms will bring pelting down rain-pours, not only that, but there is a 100% chance of Monday until midnight.

Plum

I am delighted that P.G. Wodehouse now has a memorial stone in Westminster Abbey. It has been a few editions of Wonders and Absurdities since he last appeared in quote, so I hope the following make up for it.

The Right Hon. was a tubby little chap who looked as if he had been poured into his clothes and had forgotten to say "When!"

Very Good, Jeeves, 1930

She fitted into my biggest armchair as if it had been built round her by someone who knew they were wearing armchairs tight about the hips that season.

My man Jeeves, 1919

To my daughter Leonora without whose never-failing sympathy and encouragement this book would have been finished in half the time.

The Heart of a Goof, 1926. Dedication

An absurdity and a wonder?

The 2019 awards for sporting achievement and understatement should have gone to:

Sarah Thomas, 37 years old, from Colorado, USA. She swam from Dover to Calais, Calais to Dover, Dover to Calais and Calais to Dover in 54 hours. The swim should have been 80 miles but because of the tides and currents was 130 miles.
Immediately afterwards she said: "I'm pretty tired right now."

To continue……

Understatement is something that today in our digitally connected world has too often been replaced by exaggeration or overemphasis. One only has to consider the use of such words as awesome, legend and world-class.

When the British army withdrew from Dunkirk in late May 1940, the last stages of the evacuation were commanded by General Sir Harold Alexander. He with a few staff officers and his driver, Corporal Wells, tried to make sure that everyone had been rescued.
The following account was written by Nigel Nicholson in his 1973 book 'Alex'.

As soon as it was dark on June 2nd, the remnants of the BEF began to embark on destroyers at the mole. The arrangements worked without a hitch. All men aboard by 11.40 p.m. When the destroyers sailed for Dover, Alexander, with Brigadier Parminter (the military embarkation officer), and half a dozen others including Corporal Wells, boarded a motor boat in the harbour, ordering a single destroyer to wait for them at the mole. There was no shelter on the boat from incessant gunfire. They zig-zagged out of the harbour, and then turned east parallel to the beaches for about two miles, as close inshore as the draught of the boat would allow. Twice they grounded on sand-bars. The sea, Wells remembers, was covered with a film of oil, in which were floating the corpses of many soldiers. Alexander took a megaphone and shouted over and over again, in English and French, 'Is anyone there? Is anyone there?' There was no reply. They returned to the harbour, shouted the same question round the quays, and then boarded the waiting destroyer. Unharmed they reached Dover as dawn was breaking.
When Alexander arrived in England, he reported to Anthony Eden at the War Office. 'After he had given me an account of what had passed,' Eden later wrote, 'I congratulated him, and he replied, with engaging modesty, "We were not pressed, you know."

Getting old

Hurt my tooth at breakfast-time. I look in the glass. Am conscious of the humiliating sorriness of my earthly tabernacle, and of the sad fact that the best of parents could do no better for me....
Why should a man's mind have been thrown into such close, sad, sensational, inexplicable relations with such a precarious object as his body?

Thomas Hardy

The world has fewer greater pleasures than that which two friends enjoy in tracing back, at some distant time those transactions and events which they have passed together.
One of the old man's miseries is that he cannot easily find a companion able to partake with him of the past.

Samuel Johnson

In 1783 Elizabeth Robinson wrote to the Duchess of Portland.

I will tell you what sort of man I desire, which is above ten times as good as I deserve; for gratitude is a great virtue, and I would have cause to be thankful. He should have a great deal of sense and prudence to direct and instruct me, much wit to divert me, beauty to please me, good humour to indulge me in the right, and reprove me gently when I am in the wrong; money enough to afford me more than I can want, and as much as I can wish; and constancy to like me as long as other people do, that is, till my face is wrinkled by age, or scarred by the small-pox; and after that I shall expect only civility in the room of love, for as Mrs Clive sings,

> All I hope of mortal man
> Is to love me whilst he can.

When I can meet all these things in a man above the trivial consideration of money, you may expect to hear I am going to change the easy tranquillity of mind I enjoy at present for a prospect of happiness; for I am, like Pygmalion, in love with a picture of my own drawing, but I never saw an original like it in my life; I hope when I do, I shall, as some poets say, find the statue warm.

A few of the less successful parties in the 2019 General Election

Best for Luton
Cumbria First
Gwlad Gwlad
Heavy Woollen District Independents
Lincolnshire Independents
Mebyon Kernow
Militant Elvis
Motherworld Party
No Description
Psychedelic Future Party
Space Navies Party
The Universal Good Party
Touch Love Worldwide

The most surprising result of election night?

David Warburton, sitting Tory member for Somerset and Frome.
His vote slumped from 36,231 to 36,230.
He has promised to win back the lost vote next time.

More results!

The Green Party with 865,715 votes won one seat
The DUP with 244,128 votes won eight seats
The Lib Dems with 3,696,419 votes won eleven seats
The SNP with 1,242,380 votes won forty-eight seats.

Encouraging news from the USA

During this year's Presidential election campaign, one notable participant, standing on behalf of the Libertarian Party, which is the third largest party in the country, was Vermin Supreme.

He campaigned wearing a Wellington Boot on his head and carried a large toothbrush.

If elected he intended to pass a law requiring everyone to brush their teeth, to give a pony to all Americans, instead of spending the money on the armed-forces and he is in favour of bringing real kangaroos into courts.

His campaign team advised that as all politics is now a joke, they just wanted to change the punchline.

Down-under

The questions below about Australia are from potential visitors. They were posted on an Australian Tourism website, the answers are the actual responses from the website staff.

Q: Does it ever get windy in Australia? I have never seen it rain on TV, how do the plants grow? (UK)
A: We import all plants fully grown and then just sit around watching them die.

Q: Will I be able to see kangaroos in the street? (USA)
A: Depends on how much you have been drinking.

Q: I want to walk from Perth to Sydney – can I follow the railroad tracks? (Sweden)
A: Sure, it is only 3000 miles, take lots of water.

Q: Can you give me some information about hippo racing in Australia? (USA)
A: A-fri-ca is the big triangle shaped continent south of Europe. Aus-tra-lia is that big island in the Pacific which does not... Oh forget it. ....Sure, hippo racing is every Tuesday night.

Q: Which direction is north in Australia? (USA)
A: Face south and then turn 180 degrees. Contact us when you get here and we'll send the rest of the directions.

Q: Can I bring cutlery into Australia? (UK)
A: Why? Just use your fingers like we do.

Q: I have a question about a famous animal in Australia, but I forget its name. It's a kind of bear and lives in trees. (USA)
A: It's called a Drop Bear. They are so called because they drop out of gum trees and eat the brains of anyone walking underneath. You can scare them off by spraying yourself with human urine before going out walking.

Q: Do you celebrate Christmas in Australia? (France)
A: Only at Christmas.

Q: I was in Australia in 1969 on R&R and I want to contact the girl I dated while I was staying in King's Cross. Can you help? (USA)
A: Yes, and you will still have to pay her by the hour.

Q. Are there supermarkets in Sydney and is milk available all year round? (Germany)
A. No we are a peaceful civilisation of vegan hunter-gatherers. Milk is illegal.

Q: Will I be able to speak English most places I go? (USA)
A: Yes, but you'll have to learn it first.

Out for a long walk on a cold winter's day, my favourite tissue-restorer is the King's Ginger by Berry Bros. & Rudd.

But I suspect the following would also suffice.

Sloe Gin
The clear weather of Juniper
darkened into winter
she fed gin to sloes
and sealed the glass container.
When I unscrewed it
I smelled the disturbed
tart stillness of a bush
rising through the pantry.
When I poured it
it had a cutting edge
and flamed
like Betelgeuse.
I drink to you
in smoke-mirled, blue-
black sloes, bitter
and dependable.

Seamus Heaney, Station Island, 1984

Too much information

Sir,
The room information pack in a hotel in France where I stayed with my wife demanded that on vacating the room we were to inform reception 'of all consummations made during your stay'.

Letter to The Times, September 2019

Snookered

Sir,
Watching snooker on a black and white television was a challenge, but the BBC's commentators could always be relied upon to avoid any confusion.
As the snooker commentator 'Whispering' Ted Lowe once said: "For those of you watching in black and white the pink is behind the green."

Letter to The Times, November 2018

A theatrical interruption

Sir,
Apropos interruptions at the theatre, the matinee performance of *Waiting for Godot* in Cheltenham last week was interrupted by the ringing of a phone in the audience.
 Vladimir looked at the person responsible and said "If it's Godot, keep him on."

Letter to The Times, February 2019

One touch of nature makes the whole world kin.

Shakespeare. Troilus and Cressida